of
GLASGOW

Using Questionnaires in Small-Scale Research

A BEGINNER'S GUIDE

Pamela Munn
and
Eric Drever

the **SCRE** *Centre*
research *in* education

The SCRE Centre, University of Glasgow

SCRE Publication 104

Practitioner MiniPaper (*now* Using Research series) 6

First published 1990

Revised 1995, 1999, 2004 (Reprinted 2007)

Series editors: Valerie Wilson and Jon Lewin

THE SCRE 'USING RESEARCH' GUIDES

Lewis, Ian & **Munn, Pamela** (2004) *So You Want to Do Research! A guide for beginners on how to formulate research questions.* Using Research 2.

Munn, Pamela & **Drever, Eric** (2004) *Using Questionnaires in Small-Scale Research: A beginner's guide.* Using Research 6.

Drever, Eric (2003) *Using Semi-Structured Interviews in Small-Scale Research: A teacher's guide.* Using Research 15.

Simpson, Mary & **Tuson, Jennifer** (2003) *Using Observations in Small-Scale Research: A beginner's guide.* Using Research 16.

ISBN 1 86003 086 6

The SCRE Centre, Faculty of Education, University of Glasgow, 11 Eldon Street, Glasgow G3 6NH.

Contents

A Guide to the Guide...

What are the research questions to be answered?

See Chapter 1. A fuller discussion of research questions, what they are and where they come from is contained in *So You Want To Do Research!* (Ian Lewis and Pamela Munn). Full details on page 71.

Why use a questionnaire?

The advantages and disadvantages are summarised at the end of Chapter 1.

What claims do you want to make as a consequence of your research? Are you interested only in your own school? Do you want to claim that your results are typical of, for example, first year pupils in general?

Sampling is discussed in Chapter 2. In small-scale research the whole population can often be included; for example, the staff of the school, all first year pupils you teach. The things to bear in mind about sampling are summarised at the end of Chapter 2.

How to translate research questions into questionnaire questions. Will the questions make sense to respondents?

Examples and advice on design and layout are in Chapter 3. The importance of piloting is stressed in Chapter 4.

How to analyse answers

A step-by-step guide is in Chapter 5. There is also an example of an easy-to-use statistical test. Ignore the statistics if your sample is less than 30.

And now what? How to present and use your results

What is the point of your findings? How can you present them in an interesting way? Chapter 6 gives examples of reporting and stresses the difference between description and interpretation.

1

Why Use a Questionnaire?

Questionnaires are a popular way of gathering information. It is easy to understand why. In large scale surveys, postal questionnaires are by far the cheapest way of gathering information from hundreds or thousands of people. Responses can be quantified using various sophisticated techniques and the results presented with all the confidence which number crunching brings. Is there scope for using a questionnaire in small scale research where information may be needed from, for example, the staff of a secondary school or from pupils in particular year groups? The answer is 'Yes', provided you are clear about:

- What it is you want to find out (more difficult than it sounds)
- What kind of information the questionnaire will provide.

Before discussing the advantages and disadvantages of using a questionnaire in practitioner research, let us be clear about what we mean by questionnaires. While some questionnaires are used in face-to-face interviews, we are concentrating on documents containing a number of questions which respondents have to complete by themselves. They may have to tick boxes, write in opinions or put things in order of importance. The important point is that the researcher is not usually present when the questionnaire is being filled in. We focus on this kind of questionnaire because this is the kind which teachers are most likely to use. It is unlikely that teachers will have the time or opportunity to conduct face-to-face interviews using a questionnaire. If you are using face-to-face interviews most of this book is still relevant but there is no advice about the process of interviewing. Body language, the place where the interview takes place and the way in which the interview is begun are important influences on the kinds of answers given.

1

Using Semi-Structured Interviews in Small-Scale Research, also in this series, gives useful advice on all of this. We concentrate on questionnaires which pupils, teachers, other staff, or parents are going to complete without a researcher present.

Advantages of using a questionnaire

What does using a questionnaire offer those interested in researching some aspect of their own practice or school policy? There are four main advantages for the teacher-researcher. These are:

- An efficient use of time
- Anonymity (for the respondent)
- The possibility of a high return rate
- Standardised questions.

Let us look at each in more detail.

Efficient use of time

The overriding concern in devising research questions and deciding what is most important is that the research should be feasible. It is better always to go for the small-scale project which can realistically be completed, than an over-ambitious design which falls by the wayside because of pressure of work. Questionnaires can save time in a number of ways:

- You can draft the questionnaire in your own home.
- The questionnaire can be completed by your respondents in their own time. Unlike interviews with members of staff, you do not need to match your free periods with those of colleagues.
- You can collect information from quite a large number of people at one fell swoop. For example, you might be able to arrange that all first year pupils in a secondary school completed a questionnaire in their class/tutor groups or at some other convenient time.
- If your questionnaire consists largely of closed questions (discussed in Chapter 3) analysis of responses can be straightforward. A common mistake in interviewing is underestimating the amount of time needed to analyse the range of views expressed.

In using a questionnaire most time is spent:

- Designing the questions, making sure the wording is clear
- Thinking through the categories of response to each question
- Piloting (see Chapter 4).

Administration and analysis are less time-consuming when each of the above has been done thoroughly.

Anonymity

One of the strengths of practitioners researching their own practice or school policy is that they already know a good deal about the school, the subject department, the staff and the pupils. These are areas which an outside researcher needs to spend time becoming familiar with. Such familiarity on the part of the practitioner-researcher can be a drawback, however. It may mean, for example, that things are taken for granted that ought to be questioned. There are various ways of trying to get critical distance on an issue, including discussion with a sympathetic outsider, and using existing research reports.

A potential difficulty for a practitioner-researcher is that of collecting information from people who know you. It may be that people are less likely to be frank if you are interviewing them, than if they are able to provide information anonymously. You can argue this both ways, of course. It may be that people are more willing to come clean if they know and trust you. Much depends on what it is you are trying to find out and the power relationship between you as the researcher and the respondents. Two fictitious examples make the point:

- An assistant headteacher in a secondary school wants to find out whether pupils transferring from primary to secondary are anxious about the transfer and, if so, what their anxieties are. Are pupils more likely to tell the researcher about this face-to-face or by writing about transfer anonymously?
- A headteacher wants to evaluate her management style. She wants to collect information on various aspects of her style from all staff. Is this headteacher more likely to get frank responses if they are anonymous?

If anonymity is important to you as the researcher, you need to think about ways of helping respondents remain anonymous. In a small group of staff or pupils, handwriting is an easy guide to identity. You might want, therefore, in your instructions to respondents, to suggest that they print answers if they wish; alternatively you could rely on closed questions so that ticking boxes was all respondents needed to do. Whatever you decide, the important point to remember is that questionnaires provide the possibility for anonymity that few other research techniques offer.

The possibility of a high return rate

Traditionally, one of the disadvantages of postal questionnaires is that return rates can be low. This is often because researchers are remote from their respondents and may be asking about issues of little or no relevance to them. This is unlikely to be so for the practitioner-researcher. In most cases you will be collecting information from people in your own school, where there are opportunities to remind respondents to complete the questionnaire. If you are collecting information from staff or pupils in schools other than your own, then you can plan to maximise the return rate when making decisions about how to administer the questionnaire. (See Chapter 4.) Ways of maximising return rates range from getting the school to set aside a specific time for the completion of the questionnaire, to offering a number of small prizes to questionnaires with a lucky number.

Standardised questions

In a questionnaire, all respondents are presented with the same questions. There is no interviewer coming between the respondent and the question and so there is no scope for negotiating or clarifying the meaning of the question. This is why so much care is needed in drafting questions, and why piloting is essential. Chapter 3 contains some examples of badly worded questions. The advantage of the standardised question is that you are strictly controlling the stimulus presented to all respondents. Of course, you cannot control the way in which respondents interpret the questions. However, you do know that all respondents have been presented with the same questions in the same order. This is a claim that usually cannot be made for interviewing techniques.

Limitations in using a questionnaire

We have stressed the advantages of time, anonymity, good response rates and standardised questions in using a questionnaire in small-scale research. With all these advantages, you might well ask 'Why use any other technique?' Like all techniques, questionnaires have their limitations. There are no right or wrong techniques; merely techniques that are better or worse, given the job to be done. It is important that anyone using a research method is aware of its weaknesses as well as its strengths – this leads to better understanding of the nature of the information collected.

For us, there are three main limitations in using a questionnaire, and these need to be borne in mind when deciding to use one:

- The information collected tends to *describe* rather than *explain* why things are the way they are.
- The information can be superficial.
- The time needed to draft and pilot the questionnaire is often underestimated and so the usefulness of the questionnaire is reduced if preparation has been inadequate.

Description rather than explanation

Questionnaires can provide us with good descriptive information. Let us take the example of a teacher, or group of teachers, interested in finding out about whether pupils transferring from primary to secondary are anxious about the transfer. A questionnaire could help discover:

- How many pupils entering first year secondary feel anxious about the transfer from primary
- What kinds of anxieties they have.

This could be done by asking straightforward questions and asking pupils to tick boxes, as in the example below.

> Do you feel worried about coming to secondary school? Yes ☐
> *(Please tick box)* No ☐

> Are you worried about any of these? *(Please tick the worries you have)*
> Finding your way round school ☐
> Doing new subjects ☐
> The work being too hard ☐

These are closed questions, where the respondent is forced into answering your formulation of the question. It is this approach which makes analysing the answers reasonably straightforward. You can count the numbers of pupils responding 'Yes' or 'No' and the numbers ticking the various kinds of worries you suggest. Suppose, however, that you do not want to suggest particular worries to pupils believing that this might be putting ideas into their heads. Then, you could ask an open question, such as:

> What worries you about coming to secondary school?
>
> *(Please write in)*

Here you let the pupils write in their own concerns. The disadvantage of this is that you might have 200 replies to analyse and sort into categories, thereby robbing you of the time advantages mentioned earlier. The pros and cons of different kinds of questions are discussed further in Chapter 3. For the moment we are pursuing the idea that questionnaires are good at providing descriptive information and not so good at providing explanations.

Suppose, now, that you are interested in *why* pupils have the worries that they tell you about. Clearly you might want to know this to see if there is anything to be done to alleviate them. There are two ways in which a questionnaire might be framed to get at explanations.

Asking why: You could simply ask pupils to tell you why they are worried. The disadvantage here is that pupils would probably give you brief answers which only serve to raise more questions in your own mind, such as, 'The teacher told us the work would be hard', or 'My brother said you got your head stuck down the lavatory'. Such replies are going some way towards suggesting how you might alleviate anxiety but you would need to know more before taking action. You don't know whether the teacher referred to is a primary or secondary teacher, for example. You don't know anything about the context in which the remark was made. (It could have been made to motivate, inspire or bring a disruptive class under control, for example.) As we shall see below, questionnaire data can be superficial whereas information collected from fairly open interviewing is often described as 'rich'. The point we are making here is simply that using a questionnaire to discover why things are the way they are has limitations. If you ask open 'Why?' questions you are faced with:

- A good deal of time to be spent analysing answers
- Explanations which are often superficial.

Testing a hypothesis: There is another, more time-efficient, way in which questionnaires can be used to give explanations. This is where you have a hypothesis about something and you wish to test it. Suppose your hypothesis is that differences among 12 year olds in attainment in French can be explained in terms of the sex of the pupil, exposure to a particular syllabus, or the amount of time devoted to French in class. You would then design your questionnaire to make sure that all these factors were covered. It would include questions such as the following:

Are you a boy
       girl?

In French do you use

    Tour de France

    Éclair

    Other?

How many periods of French do you have?

    4

    5

    6

    7

    more than 7

How long is a period in your school?

    30 minutes

    35 minutes

    40 minutes

    45 minutes

    more than 45 minutes

Let us, for the moment, pass over the difficulties in drafting questions (covered in Chapter 3). The example illustrates how a hypothesis about the factors affecting attainment in French can be tested using a questionnaire. You would match whatever measure of attainment you were using for each pupil against the information provided on the factors you think affect attainment.

Hypotheses about things usually come from reading, thinking, experience and intuition. If you are an experienced practitioner, you will certainly have a whole range of hypotheses about various aspects of school life, including: why some pupils attain higher scores than others; which teaching methods are better than others in a given set of circumstances; and why some policies are successful and others not. If you want to test a hypothesis using a questionnaire, you have to formulate your hypothesis in such a way that it is falsifiable. So if your hypothesis was that girls do better at French than boys do, your sample would have to include boys as well as girls.

In summary, a questionnaire can provide you with:

- Descriptive information
- Tentative explanations associated with testing a hypothesis.

In using a questionnaire, you need to be clear in your own mind about its purpose. Is it to provide you with descriptive information about a problem? For example, how many pupils are worried about coming to secondary school? Is it to test a hypothesis? such as that pupils coming from a particular primary school have particular kinds of worries and that these are due to particular factors. The purpose of the questionnaire has implications for the type of sample you use, and we discuss this in Chapter 2. It is sometimes feasible to use one questionnaire for both purposes. You may need help and advice if this is the case.

Superficiality

Another limitation of self-completion questionnaires is that they can provide you with superficial information. As mentioned earlier, there is no interviewer to interpret or explain the meaning of questions. There is, likewise, no interviewer to probe or explore answers. As a researcher, all you have to go on in interpreting your data are ticks in boxes or brief written responses. This is fine if you are clear that this is the kind of information you need but it can be disappointing if you were hoping for something more. An example from a study conducted by the authors and using questionnaires illustrates this point. The research was surveying the extent to which adults participated in education and training and the factors affecting their participation. It was therefore interested in descriptive information, ie the extent of participation. It was also interested in exploring hypotheses about factors affecting participation such as previous school experience and attainment, how useful adults saw qualifications as being in the job market, and knowledge of available opportunities.

The survey provided good descriptive information about the extent of participation. We were able to describe numbers participating in terms of their age, sex, social class and work status. This kind of information had not previously been available and so was quite useful. However, the research was of more limited value in exploring hypotheses about participation and non-participation. We were able to suggest some factors encouraging participation, but could say less about non-participation. The main reason given for non-participation was lack of interest. This piece of information is important up to a point, but it does not tell us *why* people are not interested, and is therefore of limited value to those wanting to encourage greater participation. This is a good example of a case where other research techniques are needed to follow up findings revealed by a questionnaire. In this instance, in-depth interviews with non-participants were undertaken. These interviews provided a much fuller picture of non-participants than would have been possible using a questionnaire. The trade-off was depth instead of breadth. Many fewer people could be interviewed face-to-face than surveyed by questionnaire.

Lack of preparation

Drafting and piloting a questionnaire always takes longer than you expect. Someone designing a questionnaire for the first time usually thinks it needs only an hour or so spent jotting down a few questions and that's that. As we will see in Chapters 3 and 4, time spent in careful drafting and piloting pays dividends. A well designed questionnaire yields unambiguous information and a good response rate. Sloppy drafting means that questions are ambiguous, categories are imprecise and you risk alienating your respondents. A realistic amount of time for preparing and piloting a questionnaire needs to be set aside – we would suggest at least one week, probably two, needs to be devoted to drafting, piloting and re-drafting.

Summary

There are advantages and disadvantages to using a questionnaire:

- Efficient use of time in reaching large numbers, and in analysing responses if closed questions are used.
  - But, time needs to be set aside for thinking about the purpose of the questionnaire, drafting questions, piloting.

- Standardised questions mean that there is no interviewer interpreting/distorting meaning.
  - But care needed to make questions clear. Even if they are clear, responses can be superficial.
- Good at producing straightforward descriptive information.
  - But, more difficult to get at explanations.
- Potential for anonymity.
- Potential for high return rate.

Every research technique has pros and cons and there is no simple answer to the question 'Which technique should I use?' The important thing is to weigh up the advantages of a particular method in relation to the research questions you want to ask and the claims about your findings you want to make. If your research question is about the views of pupils on some particular issue, such as the wearing of school uniform, and you want to claim that your findings are generalisable to all pupils in the secondary school, then this almost certainly suggests a questionnaire. If, in contrast, you wanted to understand why a particular teaching approach was being used with infants, you would probably use interviews and observation. As mentioned earlier, questionnaires can be used along with other ways of collecting information about an issue. In Chapter 3 we discuss this in more detail. First, Chapter 2 addresses sampling.

2

Sampling

We are all familiar with polls conducted near election time which try to predict voting patterns from information gathered from a sample of one or two thousand voters across the country. These numbers are large compared with surveys that teachers are likely to carry out, but cover only a tiny proportion of voters: less than one in ten thousand. The validity of the polls depends mainly on two things: do people's stated intentions truly reflect what they do when the time comes to vote; and does the selected sample properly reflect the general population of voters? Obviously the method of sampling is crucial.

The 'representative' sample – a misleading notion

Commonsense would suggest that if you want any sample to be representative, you should structure it carefully. You should have about equal numbers of men and women, and the right proportion of people of different ages, income groups, ethnic origins, religious beliefs and so on. Such a sample would be a deliberately constructed microcosm of the voting population: a truly 'representative' sample. Of course, you would not try to represent people of different heights or eye colours, however, since that does not seem connected with their voting intentions. But if you are concerned with factors affecting voting, then should you not build in proper representation of other factors: people in areas of high or low unemployment? where a factory or hospital has just opened or closed? where there is a local 'green' issue? and so on.

Clearly the pursuit of 'representativeness' is getting out of hand! In the attempt to find out about people's voting intentions, we are building in more and more of our own preconceived notions about the factors that influence them. If we knew all that, we would hardly need to do the research. And by creating a sample incorporating so many assumptions, we are in danger of producing results that 'prove' our own expectations.

The idea of constructing a representative sample is appealing but misleading. Instead, effort should go into defining clearly the group or groups of people that the research is interested in, after which a purely random sample can be taken from each group. To establish local headteachers' views on school management would involve listing all headteachers in the area, and selecting a predetermined number at random. To test a hypothesis that guidance teachers' views on discipline are different from those of other teachers would involve two samples, one chosen at random from all guidance teachers, and one from all teachers in other posts.

Random sampling – avoiding bias

The word 'random' upsets people. It suggests a haphazard process. Surely we should not select by chance alone? Yet that is exactly what we should do. If you think of the process as 'unbiased sampling', that may help. You are making sure that you do not bias the sampling in any way by imposing on it your own notions about the very things you are trying to find out. By choosing the sample at random, your aim is that all the natural variations within the chosen population will tend to even out, so that the sample does reflect the population from which it came. For that to happen you need fairly large numbers. Of which, more later.

The process of random sampling is entirely rigorous. First, you must define as clearly as possible the population you are interested in. Here are examples of clearly defined populations:

- Headteachers, including acting headteachers, of primary schools in Glasgow.
- People registered with the General Teaching Council for Scotland but who have not worked as teachers in the last two years.
- Pupils in a particular school with one or more unauthorised absence recorded during the previous term.

Notice that these are operational definitions: they describe how the members of the population can be identified. Anyone should be able to apply your rules and agree with you about who is eligible for inclusion.

You then acquire or create a list of all the members of the population. Then you prepare a set of random numbers corresponding to the size of sample you want, and select individuals from the list accordingly. You can select random numbers from commercially produced tables or generate them using a computer.

Random sampling is based on two principles:

- Each member of the population must have an *equal chance of being selected.*
- The chances of one being selected must be quite *independent of any other.*

These are deceptively simple. You need to be careful and apply them thoroughly. If you do, you can resolve any confusion you may have. Suppose that you have decided to send a questionnaire to parents. You discover that there are several families with more than one child in the school. Does that mean that their names should appear more than once on your list, so that they might get several questionnaires? Also there are a good many single-parent families. Is it right that they only have one 'vote' whereas other families have two? Or should you just send one questionnaire to each household irrespective of the number of parents and children? To answer these points you need to go back to your research questions: why have you selected this population? Then you apply the rules about random sampling.

For instance, your research may be about the general role of the school in the community, or more especially about the accessibility of its buildings, swimming pools and so on to parents. In that case, you are interested in the parents mainly as members of the public who happen to have a child in the school. You would assemble a list in which each father, mother or single parent appears only once. The questionnaire would go to each person selected, as an individual. While many households may get none, some may receive two, one to the father, and one to the mother. That does not matter: the fact that one parent is selected must not prevent the other from having the same chance of being chosen. On the other hand, you might be seeking parents' views on the school's careers guidance programme. You may be interested in comparing the views of parents of boys with those of girls, or those with children intending to leave school at 16 with those whose children are staying on. In this case, you are interested in these people as parents of particular children, and so you could make up a list of pupils, select from it at random, and send one questionnaire to each set of parents. You may find that sibling pupils Sandy and Sarah Thomson have both been picked. In that case you should send one questionnaire for each, naming the child, because their parents might have a different view about the careers advice given to each child.

In random sampling, each member of the sample is picked from the whole population, not just from those left after previous selections. It is possible that the same individual may be picked twice. Here you would not send two questionnaires, but you would include the data for that individual twice. This may seem strange, since many individuals are not included at all, but it is consistent with the statistical laws that decide how well a random sample represents the population. As you can see, the rules about sampling, though essentially simple, require to be followed exactly.

What size of sample?

We said previously that in choosing the sample randomly your aim is that the natural variations within the chosen population will tend to even out. For that to happen you need fairly large numbers in the sample. The more varied your population, the larger the number needed if you are to be confident about extrapolating from the sample to the population. Thus, if academic experience and ability are important factors in your study, then pupils taking Higher French in a particular school are likely to be more homogeneous than the schools' intake of first year pupils, and you could be content with a smaller sample in the former case.

Perhaps surprisingly, there are no firm rules about sample size. Most authors suggest 30 as the minimum, one reason being that with numbers below 30 the statistical formulae may have to be adapted slightly. However, with small numbers you would probably not use a structured questionnaire, and, even if you did, you would not rely on statistics to strengthen your conclusions, perhaps using some interviews to check your interpretation of your data.

So, we are not suggesting that you should become embroiled with statistics. It is helpful if you have some feeling for what the numbers involved imply about the degree of confidence with which you can report results: in other words, a grasp of what the statistical procedures make more precise and quantitative when you use them. Any random sample will be an approximate representation of the population, and if you repeated the process your next sample would be a slightly different approximation. Once you have chosen your sample, and gathered and analysed the information, you can speak with one hundred per cent certainty about the views and circumstances of the sample members. However, there will be a degree of uncertainty about how far this applies to your population as a whole. Statistical methods can be used to estimate the margin of error. Often researchers aim at '95% confidence': that is, there is only a 1-in-20 chance of the result lying outside the range they claim.

The margin of uncertainty depends entirely on the size of the sample, and not, as you might think, on whether the sample is a large proportion of the population. Thus, if 42% of people polled say they will vote Conservative, then our '95% confidence' limits are as follows:

Sample size	'95% confidence' range
100	+/– 10.0%
250	+/– 6.0%
1000	+/– 3.0%
4000	+/– 1.5%

This means that if you have a sample of 100, the 42 who said they would vote Conservative has an estimated error of plus or minus 10%. The number voting could be anywhere between 32 and 52. The chances of results lying outside that range are 1-in-20. The table above shows that the sample size needs to be increased quite substantially to reduce the margin of error significantly: a poll of 1000 would be able to claim that the range of those intending to vote Conservative lay between 390 and 450, with the same l-in-20 chance of the result lying outside this range.

Obviously the larger the sample the better. But to increase the degree of certainty twofold you will always need to increase the sample fourfold. In practice, the size of your sample will be determined largely by the amount of data you can cope with, and so we do not suggest seeking certainty by multiplying the work beyond reasonable limits. Rather, you should simply be aware of your sample's limitations and cautious in the claims you make about generalising to the whole population.

There is one exception to this general rule. If the numbers involved allow you to cover the *whole* of your target population rather than just a sample, then it is always worthwhile to do so. For example, if you have a school staff of 63, any sample worth having is going to be a majority of the teachers. Yet you will still not be able to report with 100% certainty, because you have only a sample of the 63. In that case, you should grit your teeth and include everyone.

The sampling unit

In the example used earlier in this chapter, the decision about how to sample depended on identifying the population precisely, and also the sampling unit: was it the parent *as a member of the public* or was it the parent *as the parent of a particular child?* This led back to the research questions.

Notice that the *sampling unit* is not necessarily the same as the *individual* to whom the questionnaire will be sent. In some cases, the sampling unit may be a group of people, such as a class, a department, or the whole staff of a school. It depends on what you are interested in. If you were interested in the influence of school policy on the popularity of courses, then the sampling unit would be the school. If you were interested in the influence of departmental organisation on courses, then the sampling unit would be the department. Similarly, if you think that pupils' opinions about the 'relevance' of a subject will depend on the teacher they have got, then your unit would be the teacher or teaching group. After selecting a sample of classes, you should question all the pupils in these classes. In that way you will have certainty about what each class thinks, and the differences between classes in your sample will approximate to the variation amongst classes generally.

If your sampling unit is, say, the school, then to have a decent number in the sample, ie a decent number of schools may imply taking in huge numbers of teachers, pupils or parents. One way round this is to take a sample-within-a-sample ('two-stage sampling'). You take a sample of schools, and then a sample of, say, the teachers in each school. This would leave you with a degree of uncertainty at each of the two sampling levels: these teachers are not entirely typical of that school, and these schools are not typical of all schools. Another way is to keep to a relatively small number of schools and regard each as a separate case-study, making no claim that these represent schools in general. In this situation, you might use the questionnaire only to identify some features of the schools, which you could follow up in other ways designed to reflect the individual character of each school. This leads us into a consideration of case-studies, which is outside the scope of this book.

Stratified samples

Sometimes you may believe you have a good reason to subdivide the sampling process. For example, you may feel sure that if you sample primary teachers' views about national testing, you will get different reactions from headteachers and from classroom teachers. If you simply sample teachers at random, you will find few headteachers in your sample, not enough to be confident that any differences in views are significant.

In that case, you can 'stratify' the sample. From say 200 schools you might sample 40 heads (out of 200) and 40 classroom teachers (out of perhaps 2000). You can then speak, with equal confidence, about the views of each group in turn, and draw the contrast between them. This will work very well so long as the 'theory' behind your sampling is correct (that views on educational policy vary with people's position in the hierarchy) so that there are clear differences between the groups. If you find that there are not any systematic differences, you can still say something about the views of teachers in general, but with less confidence than if you had taken one bigger random sample across the board.

The decision to stratify takes you one step back towards the notion of creating a 'representative' sample and it runs the same risk. You may choose schools, and deliberately include schools of different sizes, or with different catchment areas, or in different education authority areas. But why? Do you have a specific 'theory' or research question about the effects of size, background, or the authority's policy? Or is it just a vague sense that these things might make a difference? If it is the latter, choose at random. You may then find out that these factors are unimportant and you will not have distorted your sample in finding that out. Occasionally, there may be a compelling reason to select your subjects on a 'representative' basis rather than at random: for example, to ensure that small but influential groups are included. In such a case you may have to resort to a more elaborate process of stratification, identifying various groups and taking several members at random from each. You can report *what each group thinks,* though without confidence based on large numbers. You cannot, however, combine the groups again, because the combined groups are not then a random sample of any particular population. Any attempt to generalise is at your own risk.

Summary

This chapter sets out several rules about sampling:

- Define your population clearly, so that anyone could judge exactly who belongs within it and who does not.
- If possible, include the whole of your population in your survey, so that you can speak with certainty about their answers.
- If not, sample at random. This allows you to report with a measurable degree of uncertainty.
- The bigger your sample, the greater the certainty, but the certainty may not increase in proportion to the work involved.
- Sometimes it is permissible to depart from random sampling, but you need to be clear about your reasons for doing so.

3

Getting the Questions Right

A questionnaire should be:

- Attractive to look at
- Brief
- Easy to understand
- Reasonably quick to complete.

These features encourage respondents to complete it, and so provide you with the information you need. As we will see in Chapter 5, a low response rate makes it difficult to interpret the information you *have* got. This chapter concentrates on two main areas of designing questionnaires: drafting questions and overall design and layout.

Drafting the questions

Drafting questions is an enjoyable, interesting and frustrating process. One of the many advantages in doing research in a small group is that colleagues are readily available to argue about the merits of the wording of questions.

Before getting down to drafting individual questions, however, you must decide how many questions you will need to ask. *Needing* to ask is different from *wanting* to ask. You need to be ruthless in shedding questions that are interesting but not vital to your research. Starting with an upper limit of say 15–20 questions encourages you to think hard about which questions are really essential. Your overall research questions will help you to decide which questions must be included in your questionnaire.

Guidelines for drafting questions

Language level: Questions have to be phrased in a way that matches the vocabulary of your respondents. An inappropriate question for 12 year olds would be, 'What are the distinctive features of second-ary schools as compared with primary schools?' Much better to ask, 'How is secondary school different from primary?' You need to be careful, however, not to patronise your respondents by using language which is *too* simple. Getting the language level right is difficult and there is no substitute for discussion with colleagues about this. Appropriate piloting is also essential: a questionnaire *for* pupils should be piloted *with* pupils.

Clarity: Questions should be clear and unambiguous. Avoid double negatives and long-winded questions. Do not ask, 'Is it not unusual for you to do school work during the holidays?' Much better to ask, 'Do you usually do school work during the holidays?' Do not ask double-barrelled questions such as, 'Do you like swimming and football?' You won't know whether a response refers to either or both.

Categories of response should be clear too. It is important that the difference among categories is obvious to the respondent. Each category should be complete in itself, as in 'Yes' or 'No', where respondents are being asked to say whether or not they have done something. For example:

> Have you ever taught in a primary school?
>
> Yes ☐
> No   ☐

Clarifying categories becomes more difficult once you go beyond 'Yes'/'No'-type responses. Think about the research questions to help identify categories and be sure categories will make sense to the respondents. Suppose you are interested in finding out how computers are used in classrooms and want to suggest ways to respondents. You need to include most of the ways (to save time when analysing write-in answers) and to describe these ways in terms that respondents understand. For teachers you might ask the following:

> Do you use a computer to teach any of the following?
> *(Please tick all relevant boxes)*
>
>   Wordprocessing
>   Use of databases
>   Numerical calculations
>   Problem solving
>
>   Other *(Please write in)*

In this example, the hope is that the most usual ways of using computers have been covered. As important, however, is the language used to describe categories. If 'problem solving' is seen as similar to 'use of databases' you have no way of knowing whether respondents are ticking both these boxes or are counting problem solving using databases as 'problem solving' or 'databases'. This would obviously cast doubt on the validity of the analysis of responses. What you need to do is to pilot the questionnaire with a small number of teachers who use computers and discuss their interpretation of categories with them. (See Chapter 4.) If pupils are going to be answering the questions, use terms with which *they* are familiar to describe the categories.

Opinion questions: Be clear about the factual basis behind opinions. For instance, asking colleagues about the strengths and weaknesses of the government's proposals for in-service education assumes some knowledge of these proposals. A finding that 90% of staff approve of the proposals is pretty weak without evidence of staff's understanding of the proposals. Be clear too about whether *when* you collect opinion is important. If you want to explore the usual picture, don't collect information in unusual circumstances. For example, you wouldn't collect opinion on the government's economic policy immediately after a budget. You would collect it when nothing out of the ordinary was happening in the economy. If it is immediate reaction to the budget which is of interest, collect information as soon after the budget as possible.

Opinion questions are difficult because there are usually many aspects to an opinion. Asking about the raising of the school leaving age, for example, a respondent may be in favour, except for certain kinds of pupils, or be in favour, but object to an increased workload for the teaching staff, and so on. Be aware that respondents can conjure up an opinion about something they have never thought about before or care about. If asked, 'How should primary/secondary liaison be improved?' it would take a forceful teacher to reply, 'I don't know and I don't give a damn!' There are no easy solutions here. Be careful about wording and be aware of the limitations of answers.

Factual information questions: Are you confident that respondents have easy access to the factual information required? If respondents have to go to a lot of time and effort to collect information there are two likely effects:

- The response rate will be low: people are not prepared to go to extra effort unless the whole exercise is well set up and they are generally supportive of the research
- Respondents will guess or estimate and so cast doubt on the reliability of the information provided.

The following examples would require time and effort from all respondents:

- Number of punishment exercises given over 6 months
- Numbers of parents seen by guidance staff
- Numbers of parents attending parents' evenings.

These are perfectly legitimate areas of enquiry, but information not being readily-to-hand is a great disincentive.

Finally, asking people to remember something that took place in the distant past is chancy as memory is fallible and selective. We wouldn't use a questionnaire to ask about events more than a year or so in the past for adults; far less for children.

Are you confident that respondents will be willing to provide factual information? The advantages of anonymity were mentioned in Chapter 1, but even with this guarantee, respondents may be reluctant to give information. This is especially the case with personal information such as marital status, age, length of time in employment, future career plans. Ask yourself whether information about the personal circumstances of your respondent, adult or child, is essential. In most cases of small-scale teacher research it isn't.

Leading questions: These should be avoided. A leading question is one which points the respondent to a certain answer such as, 'National testing is a complete waste of time, isn't it?' Similarly, you need to think carefully about giving examples as these can lead an unsure respondent – 'Do you use any new teaching methods, such as resource-based learning or simulations, in your classroom?' It is better to list all the methods you are interested in and get respondents to tick boxes, or use no examples at all.

In summary, the main points to take into account before drafting questions are:

- Brevity
- Language level
- Need for clear questions and categories
- Need to establish the factual basis of opinions
- Ease of respondent's access to factual information
- Need for information about personal characteristics
- Avoidance of leading questions.

Types of question
Questions can be framed in a variety of ways.

An *open question* does not suggest categories of response, leaving respondents free to answer in a way that seems most appropriate to them. Example:

What did you like best about the course?

(Please write in)

A *closed question* suggests categories of response:

What did you like best about the course? *(Tick one box only)*

Teaching methods
Content
Meeting others in similar situations
Certification
Hospitality

Other *(Please specify)*

Even in a closed question, it is useful to include the catch-all category 'other', so that idiosyncratic views get an airing – but this is not the equivalent of an open question. There should be few responses in the 'other' box if you have done your homework and piloted the categories.

Ranked responses are another possibility:

What did you like best about the course? *(Put '1' against the thing you liked best, '2' against the next best, and so on to '5' against the thing you liked least)*

Teaching methods
Content
Meeting others in similar situations
Certification
Hospitality

However, we will see in Chapter 5 that these responses are difficult to analyse.

Scaled responses are the most obvious way of collecting opinions:

How would you rate this course? *(Please tick one box only)*

Excellent   Good   Average   Poor   Very poor

You can use a variety of ways of scaling. The way used above is to take the idea of 'goodness' and provide intervals of goodness from excellent to very poor. Another approach is to present a statement and ask whether respondents agree with it:

Teachers are badly paid *(Tick the appropriate box)*
  Agree
  Don't know
  Disagree
  Strongly disagree

Using scaled responses enables you to count how many people express certain views. You can then make a straightforward analysis which reveals how many people think a course is excellent or how many people strongly agree that teachers are badly paid. In using a scaled response in this way, you are not claiming anything about the intervals between the categories. You are not saying, for example, that the interval between 'good' and 'average' is the same as the one between 'average' and 'poor'. Considerations such as these are necessary in attitude measurement. This is quite a different business (explained more fully in Moser and Kalton's *Survey methods in social investigation* – details on page 71).

Question order
The order in which you ask questions is important. You need to consider the following:

- Begin with open questions (if you present closed questions first, respondents are in the framework you have set by the time they reach open questions and so the questions are not really open).
- Begin with questions which are straightforward and easy to answer.
- Questions about personal circumstances are better placed towards the end. By then you have engaged the respondent's attention and she/he may be more likely to complete the questions. You risk antagonising the respondent by plunging straight into sensitive and personal questions.

Check that your routing procedures do not exclude respondents from answering questions you intended them to answer.

Overall design and layout

Word-processing makes it relatively straightforward to produce an attractive design. And remember to include the most simple things. Important points to include regardless of how the questionnaire is produced are:

- The title of the questionnaire
- The name and address of the person to whom it should be returned
- The date by which it should be returned.

All this information is worth putting on the front sheet even if you intend to give out the questionnaires yourself, let us say, to a class you teach. Things can get lost; someone may unexpectedly help you in administering the questionnaire; you may want to use a slightly revised version on a later occasion and so you need a reference date. Other straightforward design points are:

- Leave a reasonable amount of space between the questions (questions cramped together look unattractive)
- Leave a column on the right hand side for coding replies.

The page of your questionnaire should look something like this:

	Office use only
Q1 Which primary school did you attend?	
Please write in here	
Q2 Were you worried about coming to secondary school?	
Please tick box	
Yes ☐	
No ☐	

It is also helpful to divide up your questions into sections with their own headings. This helps the look of the questionnaire and can encourage the respondent to see the overall logic of the design. An example dealing with primary / secondary liaison directed at staff could be:

Section 1: *Your involvement in primary/secondary liaison*

Section 2: *Strengths and weaknesses of current arrangements*

Section 3: *Future developments.*

This brief example also highlights several other points. The first is that your instructions to respondents should be brief and clear. Tell them exactly, but politely, what it is you want them to do. Secondly, if the instructions can be in a different typeface from the questions, this can help the look of the questionnaire and makes instructions stand out. Thirdly, it is usual to give some brief instructions at the start of the questionnaire, rather in the way that candidates are given instructions in examinations. For example:

All the instructions in this questionnaire have been written in italics to help you distinguish them from the questions.

Please ignore the numbers in brackets throughout this questionnaire. They are there for administrative purposes only.

When going through the questionnaire, please put a tick in the box corresponding to your answer, like this:

Yes
No
Don't know

Sometimes you are asked to write the answer in the space provided.

Finally, you may want to write a brief covering letter. If you are giving out the questionnaire yourself to a group of pupils, you need to rehearse how you will introduce it. Whether you use a letter or a verbal introduction the following should be borne in mind:

- Brevity – a short explanation about the purpose of the questionnaire is sufficient
- Importance – say briefly why it is important that people fill in the questionnaire

• Confidentiality – be frank about this. If questionnaires are numbered, explain why.

For example:

> *I am doing some research on pupils coming from primary to second-ary school. I am very interested in what pupils think about transfer. If we are going to make things better for next year it is important to find out what you think. Please fill in this questionnaire. You do not need to put your name on it and no one will see what you have written except me. Thank you for your help.*

Clearly you would pitch the language at a level appropriate to your respondents. It is also important to let parents know you are involving pupils in research. A letter asking them to let you know if they do not want their child to take part is courteous and can avoid misunderstandings.

Summary

This chapter has concerned various aspects of designing a clear questionnaire. We have discussed:

• Things to bear in mind when drafting questions:
  - Brevity
  - Factual basis of opinions
  - Clarity
  - Ease of access to factual information
  - Language level
  - Timing
  - Avoiding leading questions
  - Whether personal details are vital
  - Asking one question only at a time
• Types of questions
  - Open
  - Closed
  - Ranked responses
  - Scaled responses
• Question order
• Question routes

- Overall design and layout, stressing the need for an attractive, clutter-free design.

Much of the work of drafting questionnaires is trial and error. Working through a couple of drafts with a colleague or two can be very helpful. What is essential is to pilot the questionnaire before using it for real. Do not waste all the time and effort that has gone into constructing the questionnaire by skimping on piloting. We cannot stress enough how essential piloting is. Chapter 4 discusses how to pilot efficiently.

4

Using the Questionnaire

Once you have agonised over the construction of the questionnaire, writing and rewriting questions, you will probably be convinced that it is as near perfect as possible and will be eager to use it. But there is one further step: piloting. If you omit this stage you may find much of your effort wasted.

Books about research use the term piloting to refer to two rather different processes. Small-scale piloting refers to a relatively informal exercise of trying out the questionnaire to see how it works and to get the 'bugs' out of the questions. This should *always* be done, whether or not large-scale piloting is to follow. Large-scale piloting refers to a complete 'dry run' on quite a large scale including a detailed analysis of the responses. This is important in certain circumstances, such as: in a large-scale survey which aims at subtle statistical comparisons across a number of years or between various groups and subgroups; in a PhD study in which one must demonstrate methodological rigour; or if the questionnaire is intended to become a standard one used by other researchers. In such cases, the aim is to simulate the real thing as closely as possible, using a similar population, sampling in the same way (though with smaller numbers) and setting up the same conditions for administration and responding. It is not uncommon to run the pilot one year and the study proper exactly a year later. If you feel that such large-scale piloting is appropriate to your work, then standard texts such as Moser and Kalton (details on page 71) contain a wealth of advice.

However, this guide is aimed at research of a more modest kind. It is intended for teachers who are researching aspects of their own practice and circumstances, seeking the views of immediate colleagues, parents or pupils. They are looking for a reliable and fairly robust picture on which to base decisions and make changes over a fairly short time-scale. The questionnaire, once designed, is not intended as a high-tech instrument to be added to other researchers' armoury. At most it might prove useful to a colleague in another school or local authority.

Piloting

There are good reasons why piloting is important. By the time you and your colleagues have lived with the questionnaire for some weeks you have come to know exactly what you mean by every question. It is very difficult for someone so closely involved to imagine how respondents might interpret it differently, when they encounter it for the first time. It is only when the returns come in that you may realise that some respondents have misunderstood what was meant. Once the questionnaire has been sent out it is out of your control, and little can be done to put things right unless by dropping some questions from the analysis. Having to drop some *respondents* altogether, risks distorting the sample.

So, small-scale piloting is essential. It involves getting a few individuals to work through the questionnaire in your presence and then talk it over with you. This has several purposes. First, you want to find out roughly how long the questionnaire takes to answer, and whether there are any features of it that are likely to put people off and so reduce the likely response rate. Second, you want to 'debug' the questions. Is the wording clear, and the terminology familiar and unambiguous? Further, do people see the questions as important and interpret them as you expect? Finally, is it easy for them to express their answers to their satisfaction, and for you to interpret them correctly?

Picking your pilots

In choosing people for the piloting the aim is to get the maximum of useful feedback as readily as possible. Choose individuals who are likely to be sympathetic to your work but willing to give forthright comments and sharp criticism: you want to test your questions out as thoroughly as possible before you risk sending them out to respondents. Avoid anyone who was involved in preparing the questionnaire or who has any 'inside knowledge' of it. Also avoid anyone to whom it will be sent in the study itself. Ideally, you want people who are members of your target population but not of your sample. When that is not possible, choose others who are broadly similar and have access to the same kind of information and experiences that you are interested in – for example if you are going to survey all the staff in your own school, you could pilot with teachers from a neighbouring school.

Working it through

In piloting, it is best to work with people individually, making sure there is plenty of time for the exercise. Ask them to work through the questionnaire while you watch to see how they go about it. Encourage them to mention any points at which they have difficulty but do not offer help. Time them, and ask for their general impressions when they have finished. Then go through each question in turn, checking what they thought it meant and what they meant by their response. If they had any problems, discuss how the questions might be improved, making notes on the spot. Piloting with colleagues is probably easier to arrange than with pupils or parents. Nevertheless, it is important to pilot your questionnaire with people similar to those who are going to be completing it. Sometimes colleagues in other schools can help with access to pupils, and friends and neighbours are often suitable 'parent' pilots.

How much piloting?

How many people should you involve in the piloting? The general idea is to keep on until you think you have learned all that you can, or need, to know. You will probably give the questionnaire in its original version to two or three people. If they have all picked up much the same points, you may redraft it to take account of these. If each comments on different things you should try it with one or two more until you feel you have exhausted the full range of likely comments. After redrafting, you should pilot again with fresh people. This time you should find that few points arise, and can give the questionnaire its final polishing before using it. If there are still significant comments, you may need to reconsider your overall approach to the questionnaire, or indeed whether the topic lends itself to a questionnaire rather than an interview which might accommodate different points of view more easily.

The process of redrafting after piloting deals with points similar to those discussed in Chapter 3, mostly by adjustments to the wording to remove ambiguous and misleading phrases. You may have found that people have different terms for the same thing (one school's 'Board of Studies' may be another's 'Management Team') and you may decide to use both terms throughout. Sometimes the same term suggests different things (by a 'progressive' primary curriculum, are we implying 'child-centredness' or 'continuity'?) and you may want to add an explanatory phrase when the word is first used. Many misunderstandings can be pre-empted by a brief explanation at the start of the questionnaire.

Administering the questionnaire effectively

In thinking about administration of your questionnaire you should remember your reasons for choosing to collect information in this way, and the advantages and disadvantages discussed in Chapter 1.

In a questionnaire survey, the aim is to get standardised information by offering everyone the same stimulus: the same question presented in the same way, so that any variety in the answers is a true reflection of variety of views and circumstances among the respondents. Sometimes you can ensure this by distributing the questionnaire personally to classes or to teachers at a formal gathering such as an in-service course.

You also want to get the best possible response rate. It helps if respondents see some advantage to themselves in completing the questionnaire; for example, if it serves as something they would have to do anyway, such as a school self-evaluation exercise, or as a stimulus before a school-based continuing professional development (CPD) session. (Of course their responses in such cases may be coloured by their attitudes to school self-evaluation or school-based CPD.) In one project, surveying pupils, the researchers entered the numbers on returned questionnaires in a prize draw and the winner got a book token. This proved an effective way of maximising the return rate.

If you cannot distribute the questionnaire in person, then do what you can to control the way in which the exercise is presented to respondents and the circumstances in which they complete it. For example, if colleagues offer to help distribute a questionnaire to pupils, they will need guidance on how to present it. Even if the questionnaire itself makes a good appeal for co-operation, the spoken presentation and the attitude of the presenter can have a marked effect on how questionnaires are completed. Similarly, it may be very economical to arrange to distribute the questionnaire through the local authority's own communication network, or by sending one package to the headteacher containing questionnaires for each member of staff and a single large envelope for the returns. However, you may not want to give the impression that you are working for the employers, or to appear to rely too much on the headteacher's discretion! Regardless of how you get them there, questionnaires should always reach respondents in a sealed envelope, preferably addressed to them by name, and containing an envelope in which they can seal their reply. Indeed, unless cost is an overwhelming consideration, it is worth spending money to save your own valuable time by ensuring a good return rate: people are more likely to return a questionnaire (and promptly) if it comes to them on good quality stationery and carries a first class stamp on their reply envelope.

With every questionnaire there should be an accompanying letter of not more than one page, covering a number of points such as the following:

Who are you and what are you interested in?

I am a principal teacher of guidance dealing with third and fourth year pupils and I am interested in patterns of school non-attendance including truancy that appear to be condoned by parents.

Why have you contacted this person and what do you want them to do?

I am writing to you as someone involved in the 5–14 Development Project at local level, to ask if you would complete the enclosed questionnaire and return it in the envelope provided, by 10 March.

Why are you doing this research and for whom?

This is a personal piece of research and is not carried out as part of any course that I am taking, or on behalf of any official body.
(So should you have written it on school notepaper?)

A guarantee of confidentiality and a promise of feedback.

Your reply will be read only by myself and treated in confidence in any reporting of the work. I shall send you a brief summary of my research once it is completed (probably by September) and hope that you will find it helpful in your work.

The tone throughout should be friendly but businesslike. If the questionnaire is going to people's homes it is a good idea to mail it on Thursday so that they get it in time for the weekend; if to their school or business address, post at the start of the working week to arrive during the week. Set a clear deadline so that they have about ten days to reply.

Chapter 2 stresses the importance of getting a high rate of return from your original sample. That is much preferable to choosing a too-large sample in the expectation of low returns, and you should certainly not start adding in extra people afterwards to bring up the numbers.

Allow at least another week before taking any follow-up action. A follow-up letter should be neither whingeing nor threatening:

As part of a research study I am doing on how pupils travel to school, I sent you a questionnaire on 15 February. So far I have not received a reply and so I am sending you another copy in case the first has gone astray. I shall be very grateful for your reply as I am keen to ensure that my survey is complete before beginning my analysis of the information. If there is any reason why you feel you cannot complete the questionnaire could you please sign and return it anyway? If you wish to discuss it I can be contacted at...

Further postal follow-up is subject to the law of diminishing returns, and if you are concerned to get complete coverage a telephone call may be more helpful. There could be interesting reasons why some people have chosen not to reply, and it may be helpful to find out something about these, so that you can gauge whether the responses you have received are typical of the population, and whether your 'silent minority' is a significant group whose views should be sought in some other way.

Summary
Much of this chapter has been a warning against short cuts and false economies. In particular it has stressed:

- The importance of small-scale piloting, using people who will be sympathetic but critical
- The need to redraft questions – nobody gets it absolutely right first time
- The need to think about how the questionnaire will be administered, bearing in mind that you want standardised responses; that is, you want to do what you can to standardise the conditions in which the respondent will read and reply to your questions.

Chapter 5 discusses ways of analysing the information you have collected.

5

Analysing the Results

This series of research guides keeps coming back to the notion
that the decisions to be made at various stages during a piece of
research are all interconnected. They stem largely from the initial
selection of research questions to be investigated. In the present
case, these questions will have influenced your decision to use a
questionnaire in the first place and the style and content of the
items that you have put into it.

You may be mainly interested in straightforward description
of how things are. (How many primary classrooms have their own
computers? How many pupils think that their science worksheets
are easy or difficult to follow?) Here your main aim is to create
a summary of the general picture. On the other hand you may
want to test some hypothesis: for example, that the effect of having
adult learners in the class will be viewed quite differently by the
teacher, by the pupils, and by the adult learners themselves. In that
case your analysis will focus on the contrasts between the groups
and show whether there is a real difference between them. These
different purposes will shape your approach to your data, and so
you should have developed some idea of how you are going to
process the results long before you find yourself sitting in front of
(let's hope!) a large pile of completed questionnaires.

There are three main stages in analysing questionnaires. The
first is data preparation. You do not want to be continually leafing
through piles of responses as you try to make sense of what you
have found, and so you need to put the data into a form that is easy
to work with. Usually this means a grid in which the replies from
each respondent occupy a separate horizontal row. The second
stage is the data description, in which you work from your grid,
counting the responses in the different categories, calculating

proportions and possibly applying some statistical tests. The third stage is interpretation of the results. In Chapter 6 we describe this as answering the 'So what?' question. Once you have counted up responses, what do the numbers mean? What is their importance? This chapter concentrates on the first two of these stages.

Data preparation

Time spent on careful data preparation is time well spent. It reduces the risk of errors and increases your confidence in the overall analysis if you know you have an accurate and systematic description of the data. The overall aim in data preparation is to make the mass of information you have in your questionnaires more manageable. You want to translate the 'raw' data onto a grid – a few sheets of squared paper, or a computer spreadsheet – so that you can see what people's answers are to particular questions without leafing through a huge pile of questionnaires. There are two main stages in data preparation: preparing the grid, and coding the questions. We deal with each in turn.

Preparing the grid

A grid (for up to 99 respondents) will look something like this:

Respondent ID#	1	2	3	4	5	6	7	8	9	10
01										
02										
99										

The horizontal numbered lines are columns for recording answers to your questions. As we shall see, you can have one column or as many columns as you need to record the answers to a particular question. We saw in Chapter 3 that it is usual to allocate numbers to particular questions when designing the questionnaire. Each horizontal line will represent the answers of one respondent to your questions. If we had a simple code, such as B='Boy' and G='Girl', Y='Yes' and N= 'No', the grid might look as follows:

	1	2	3	4	5	6	7	8	9	10
	B	Y	Y	Y	N	N	Y	N	N	N
	B	Y	Y	Y	Y	N	N	N	N	N
	B	N	Y	Y	Y	N	N	Y	N	N
	G	Y	Y	Y	N	Y	N	N	N	N
	G	Y	Y	Y	N	Y	N	N	N	N

The answers of all respondents

←————— The answers of one respondent —————→

You can see at a glance that the grid tells you about the responses of 3 boys and 2 girls (Column 1). Column 2 tells you that for the question allocated this column, there were four who answered 'Yes' and one who answered 'No'. This question might have been, 'Do you walk to school?' By adding up each column you get the numbers saying 'Yes' and 'No' to each question.

The following tips may be helpful:

• If working on paper, use large sheets of feint-ruled squared paper that easily accommodates your writing if you are using letter codes; and use pencil (so you can easily delete mistakes)
• Leave blank rows (horizontal blank) between every 5 respondents to make it easier to read
• Leave blank columns (vertical blank) between groups of questions, to make it easier to read
• If you know you are going to compare groups, boys and girls for example, enter the data in these groups. In the example above the boys are entered and then the girls.

Preparing a grid is easy and straightforward. Before you can begin filling it in, you need to code the data. The amount of time and effort required is dependent on whether you are coding closed or open questions.

Coding the data: closed questions

Closed questions are the easiest and quickest to code. The categories of response are preset and all that is needed is to give each category a letter or number. (If you intend using a computer statistical package, now is the time to check whether the software uses numbers or letters. See p.47.) Whether you choose numbers or letters as codes, you should be aiming at the simplest and most direct scheme possible. As illustrated in the section on preparing a grid, a 'Yes'/'No'-type response could be coded naturally as 'Y' or 'N'; 'Boy'/'Girl' becomes 'B' or 'G'. If people have to choose one of 5 response categories, you would code each category 1 to 5 or A to E. Even where more complex forms of closed question are used, the same principle of simple coding applies. If people are offered five response categories and asked to tick as many as they wish then this can be coded as five separate 'Yes'/'No' items, using a column for each. For example, asking the question:

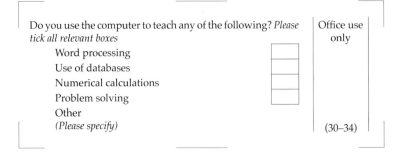

The 'office use only' section is a reminder of the column number for each category. So the grid for five responses might look like this:

		Word processing 30	Use of databases 31	Numerical calculations 32	Problem solving 33	Other 34
	1	Y	Y	N	Y	N
	2	Y	Y	Y	N	N
Teacher	3	Y	Y	N	N	Y
	4	N	Y	Y	N	N
	5	Y	Y	N	Y	N

Here column 30 = 'wordprocessing'; 31 = 'use of databases'; and so on. You record whether people use the computer for the purpose specified by inserting 'Y' for 'Yes' and 'N' for 'No'. Your grid shows that four out of five teachers use the computer for wordprocessing; five out of five use it to demonstrate the use of databases; two out of five use it for numerical calculations; two out of five use it to teach problem solving; and one uses it for another purpose.

Similarly, if people were asked to rank five factors in order of importance or preference, then you would record five numbers, the ranks given to the factors in the order in which they are listed in the questionnaire. To take the example from Chapter 3:

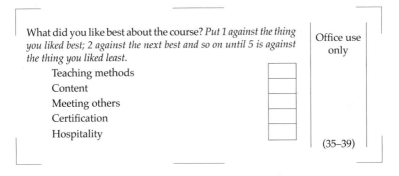

Teacher	*Teaching methods* 35	*Content* 36	*Meeting others* 37	*Certification* 38	*Hospitality* 39
1	1	3	4	2	5
2	2	4	3	1	5
3	1	2	4	5	3
4	2	1	3	4	5
5	1	3	5	2	4

The grid tells you that the first respondent ranked teaching methods first; content third; meeting others fourth; certification second; and hospitality fifth. Looking at column 35, you can see that three of your five respondents ranked teaching methods first and that the remaining two ranked them second; and so on for each column.

Some closed questions have an open category. In the question about computers there was a category *'Other: Please write in'*. Here the general approach would be to inspect the first batch of returned questionnaires, list the responses to these categories and allocate codes to the various answers. In the computers example people might write in 'Teamwork' which you could code as '1' or 'Desktop publishing' which you could code as '2' – you need to make a judgement about how many categories under 'other' you are going to have. In making a judgement, you need to remind yourself about the research questions and how you intend to use the information. If it is important to record all uses of the computer and the frequency of mention of all uses, then a code is needed for each category mentioned under 'other'. If your interest is primarily in the categories you have specified, perhaps only one or two codes are needed, or even no code beyond 'Other'.

Coding the data: open questions

Since closed questions are so much easier to handle, why use open ones? The main reason is that you may want the respondents to select what they want to tell you without much prompting. You then need a framework to organise a fairly miscellaneous set of answers. There are two main approaches: you can create a framework in advance, or you can derive it from the data. Whichever approach you adopt, the end result is the same as for closed questions – transferring numbers or letters onto a grid.

Preset categories: You can develop a set of categories from relevant books and articles or from your own 'theory' about the kinds of answers you can expect. This approach has some advantages:

- The framework can be closely linked to your research questions
- You can get others to comment on whether it is clear and logical without their having to read the questionnaires
- It is not restricted to what people tell you but can include categories that they ignore.

For example, in one study teachers were asked about the benefits of resource-based learning and their answers were classified according to four main possibilities derived from the literature. The categories were:

A – It allows pupils to control their own learning
B – It helps teachers cope with mixed-ability classes
C – It improves performance on traditional (cognitive) learning
D – It leads to new kinds of learning (skills or processes).

The great majority of responses fell into Category B; surprisingly, little was said about C.

Categories derived from the data: Alternatively, you can take a batch of responses, preferably including some of the longest ones. Summarise each into a few simple statements: you may want to write each statement on a separate card. Then try to group similar statements together, decide what they have in common, and so define the categories into which you think the answers naturally fall. This too has advantages:

- You have not imposed your own interests on the data
- You can get someone else to sort the statements to check that your framework is sensible
- You can aim to include everything that is in the responses.

For example, English teachers were asked about the aims of teaching this subject in the early years of secondary school. The responses fell into five categories:

A – Encouraging self expression
B – Transmitting basic skills
C – Appreciation of literature
D – Interest and enjoyment
E – Consolidation of primary work.

Teachers often gave more than one answer, usually in different categories, and often expressed as a balance between contrasting aims. By having a separate column for each category, this would be taken into account in describing the data.

Completing the analysis

Once your categories are fixed, you can create a coding scheme and apply it, transferring the results to the grid. You should check the reliability of your coding by having someone else code a sample according to your instructions. Coding open questions is more time-consuming than coding closed questions because you need to spend time developing the coding system and checking its reliability.

Dealing with problem responses

Most people will answer all the questions in the way that you requested. However, some may miss out a question or even a whole page, others may score out questions or otherwise indicate that they don't know or are unwilling to answer. When coding, it is as well to record something in these cases, so that every square in your grid will be filled.

You may want to distinguish between a missing answer (perhaps coding this 'M') and a refusal or 'don't know' (code as 'R' or 'D'). The reason for doing this is that at a later stage you will be calculating the proportions of responses in various categories, and the number of missing items will reduce the total that you use in your calculations. However, you may not want to treat refusals to answer or 'don't know's as 'missing' in the same way.

Other people will ignore your instructions and may perhaps choose several options instead of only one as you intended, or rank only some of the options offered rather than all of them. You can decide whether to omit these as 'missing data' or make the best interpretation that you can, keeping a note of your decisions to ensure consistency.

It will be seen that what we are suggesting as a coding process is one of transcription rather than interpretation. The details of the response are all retained more or less intact so that you don't have to go back to the original questionnaire forms. The whole process is quite straightforward. You are recording information but not evaluating it. You are doing no more than making the information more manageable. It doesn't matter if one question occupies five columns and another question only one.

Should you use a computer?
Moser and Kalton, in one of the standard reference books on survey work, suggest that for 100 to 200 cases there is little advantage in machine processing.

Our experience is that most teachers who are involved in questionnaire studies can get everything that they need from their data using nothing more than pencil and paper and a simple calculator. Inspecting the data on a grid, though it may seem tedious, is probably quicker than trying to put it through a computer, especially if you have to learn to use a statistics package from scratch.

Looking at the data on the grid can help you to become familiar with it and alerts you to patterns in a way which pressing a button never does. Besides, the number- crunching programs used in large surveys are mostly irrelevant to the kinds of data dealt with in smaller-scale studies, and the simple statistical tests that do apply are best used selectively, on the results of the pencil and paper processing.

If you are thinking of using statistical software to process your results you should be aware that some programs may treat data differently when it is coded as letters and when it is coded as numbers. In addition, various packages have different rules about making allowances for missing data.

Describing the data

Data preparation is tedious but it requires only care and no special technical skills. The same applies to describing the data. Mostly, it is a matter of counting the number of times each code appears on a column and checking that all the respondents are accounted for. Sometimes you may want to scan two columns simultaneously to look for particular combinations of responses, and this is where good layout will pay off. (See *'Preparing the Grid'*, above.)

Interpreting the data

It is at the next stage – interpreting your column totals – that you need to be disciplined, and careful to avoid over-interpretation. Here are some suggestions that may help:

- Do not read anything into the data that is not literally there.
- When in doubt look at the question you actually asked.
- Don't infer anything about the motives of respondents for giving a particular answer.
- Don't treat people's opinions about something as if they were attributes of the thing itself. (If people prefer raspberry yoghurt to plain, that tells you something about the people's taste not the yoghurt. Next week they may have changed their minds even though the yoghurt is no different.)
- Remember that you are not involved in measuring anything, merely counting the number of responses in different categories. How do these suggestions apply to different types of questions?

Questions offering two or more options

In a straightforward two-option ('Yes'/'No'-type) or multiple-option question, you can look at the totals for each option, and perhaps calculate the proportions or percentages choosing each. Remember that these are proportions of those who answered that question. For example, in one study 356 returned the questionnaire about their course but only 319 answered a question about course content. 128 said they found it 'very easy'. That is 40% (128/319); not 36% (128/356). Here, the proportion who did not answer the question is rather high. It is always possible that those who avoid answering are different in some way from those who do answer. In this case, they might be pupils who find the course difficult, which could make a big difference to the overall pattern. It is worthwhile looking at the answers these 'missing' pupils made to other questions (about whether they enjoyed the course or thought they would do well in the subject) to see if there is any sign that they are different from the rest. You can then suggest something about a possible underestimate of pupils finding the course difficult.

If your interest is in general description, then giving proportions is probably enough. However, you may want to test a prediction or explore a pattern that you have found. For example, you may hypothesise that teachers' satisfaction with various aspects of promotion procedures will be closely linked to their own level within the promoted hierarchy. In that case, you may calculate the proportions expressing satisfaction separately for *promoted* and *unpromoted* staff. Similarly, you may have asked teachers their views on the introduction of computer-aided learning (CAL): Do they accept the various aims and recommendations? How much continuing professional development (CPD) have they had and did they find it helpful? Here you may have a general research question in mind:

- Is computer-aided learning CPD effective in communicating the CAL philosophy?

And so you might decide to turn that into a specific question about your data:

- Do teachers who express satisfaction about the aims of CAL also express satisfaction about computer-aided learning CPD?

To check this, you would count combinations of responses to questions about aims and to questions about CPD, putting them in four categories:

A – People who accept the aims and find CPD helpful
B – People who accept the aims but find CPD unhelpful
C – People who reject the aims but find CPD helpful
D – People who reject the aims and find CPD unhelpful.

If the numbers in Categories A and D are large compared with those in B and C, then there is probably a connection between CPD and acceptance of CAL aims. But what is that connection? Which comes first – acceptance of the aims, or enjoyment of the CPD? Maybe CPD creates enthusiasm for CAL; or maybe only enthusiasts apply for CPD courses, or are allowed to go on them. (Or maybe we are just dealing with happy souls who tend to enjoy most things about their work!) The general point is that you cannot tell whether there is a cause-and-effect relationship, or in which direction it works. All you can say, is that people who state or choose X tend also to state or choose Y. Be careful about this in wording your conclusions: 'Teachers who approve of CAL aims are more likely to find computer-aided learning CPD useful' implies more than the data justifies.

Questions allowing several choices: Let's look at a different type of question in which people are allowed to choose as many options as they want.

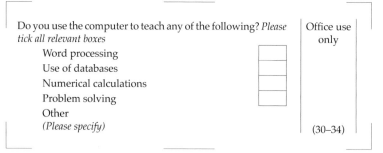

Here you will be able to report the proportion of teachers using machines for each purpose. But what if some teachers have ticked only one purpose and others have ticked several? Is this 'fair'? Some people have had two or three votes: aren't they over-represented in the results? Again, let's look at the question, and the reason for asking it. You are only aiming at an indication of how widespread each use is: how many people ever use their machines in this way. You are not trying to measure this usage, nor to conduct a popularity poll. In such cases, you would have had to ask the question differently, such as, 'For what purpose is the computer most useful?'

Questions using a 'scale': Another type of question makes use of a five-point 'scale'.

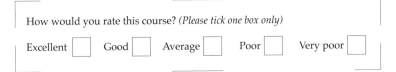

How would you rate this course? *(Please tick one box only)*

Excellent ☐   Good ☐   Average ☐   Poor ☐   Very poor ☐

Once again you can report the number, proportion or percentage of people choosing each category. But could you do more? Could you say that the average rating (say, for the content of a CPD course) was 2.3? Or, could you total up an individual's overall score across all the aspects of the course?

Neither of these is legitimate. Both procedures depend on assuming that you are working on an evenly-spaced scale so that 'very poor' is twice as bad as 'poor' and cancels out two 'good's or one 'excellent', and that in turn suggests that you are measuring something about the course. You are not: you are only counting the number of people who expressed a particular view. And if you start totting up total scores, you are also implying that each aspect is equally important. You have no reason to suppose that the people you have asked think this is so. If you want to know their overall view of the course, why not just ask that as a separate item?

Questions involving ranking: A similar type of question is one which asks people to rank items in order of importance or preference. This forces them to discriminate in a way which they may not do normally. This may be useful in exploring choices and decisions they might make, rather than opinions or degrees of satisfaction. (For example, to ask pupils to rank their subjects from strongest to weakest gives you different information from asking them how they are getting on in each subject on a five-point 'scale'.)

What did you like best about the course? *Put '1' against the thing you liked best; '2' against the next best, and so on, to '5' against the thing you liked least.*

Office use only

Teaching methods

Content

Meeting others

Certification

Hospitality

(35–39)

Once again, there is a temptation to do too much with the data. You can as usual state how many, or what proportion of respondents rank an item in first, second or third place but to calculate 'average ranks' for each item implies that these ranks form an evenly-spaced scale, and there are no grounds for this, since even the discrimination involved in ranking is artificial. One tactic that may be useful is to combine rank categories: if we had nine different items, we might collapse ranks 1, 2 and 3 into 'high'; 4, 5 and 6 into 'middle' and 7, 8 and 9 into 'low'. We can also cross-reference items: do people who make the same first choice also agree on their second choice?

So far, we have been concentrating on counting up the responses to open or closed questions on the basis of a coding system. We have stressed that this coding system should be simple. We have discussed some of the pitfalls of reading too much into the data, pointing out the limited information to be derived from rank-order type questions. Suppose, however, that you want to compare responses in two columns, or that you want to know whether the numbers answering 'Yes' or 'No' to a particular question are significant. Are there techniques you can use easily? We now briefly turn to the often-vexed question of the use of statistics.

Do you need statistics?

Over the years we have worked with a large number of teachers who are doing research either for a degree or simply to follow up some professional interest. One of their main worries is whether they will have to learn statistics.

The answer is that it depends. There are many types of research which do not need statistics, and, especially if you are working on a small scale, statistics may be irrelevant. If you are using a question-naire to collect information from a sizeable number of respondents: (say, several classes of 30, a secondary staff of 60, or the 90 primary headteachers in a local authority area), statistical tests can be useful. The other point that makes questionnaires suitable for statistical treatment is that they yield standardised information. Everyone responds to the same questions, so that any variation lies only in the responses. Interview data may not meet this condition.

One reason that people lack confidence about statistics is that it is a branch of mathematics. A lot of books seem to parade this fact, filling their pages with symbols and derivations of formulae. Yet what matters is not whether you know how to calculate a correlation or standard deviation but whether you know why you might want to do so, and in what circumstances it would be legitimate. A second point is the general suspicion that statistics are a way of manipulating and distorting evidence: 'You can prove anything with statistics'. Surely, our results should 'speak for themselves'? The point is that they don't: people have to interpret the results, and statistics provide a way of disciplining that interpretation. You may be looking for a connection or a difference between two sets of responses. You need to convince yourself that you are not exaggerating the importance of a trivial effect just because you wanted to find it. Statistics allows you to do this, and to convince others, especially if they understand some statistics themselves.

If you think you might want to use statistics then it is important to build in that possibility from the start, especially by choosing your sample by random selection. (See Chapter 2.)

What kind of statistics?
As we have already pointed out, the kinds of questionnaires we have been describing are not measuring anything against a scale but simply counting the people who give a particular response. This means that averages, standard deviations and correlation coefficients don't apply. Non-parametric tests can, however, be

used. We introduce the commonest of these – the chi-squared (χ^2) test – below, working through a single practical example.

The chi-squared test: You are interested in pupils' anxieties about transfer to secondary school and have given a questionnaire to pupils who will be entering your school next term. You have several questions in mind:

- How widespread is anxiety?
- What are pupils anxious about?
- Are boys or girls more likely to be anxious?
- Are they likely to be anxious about different things?
- Does it vary across the associated primary schools?

Here are some results:

	Anxious Boys	(Total Boys)	%	Anxious Girls	(Total Girls)	%
Primary A	6	(26)	23	4	(21)	19
Primary B	10	(21)	48	7	(15)	47
Primary C	8	(9)	89	14	(14)	100
Primary D	4	(4)	100	9	(10)	90
Primary E	11	(13)	85	1	(1)	100
Primary F	5	(8)	63	11	(12)	92
Totals	44	(81)		46	(73)	154

The table suggests that girls are more likely to be anxious than boys: 46 out of 73 against 44 out of 81. But is this significant? Have you shown that gender and anxiety are related?

You can test this by creating a contingency table and performing a chi-squared test. What this test does is to start by supposing that there is no difference between boys and girls as far as 'transfer anxiety' is concerned. In that case, how many anxious and non-anxious pupils would be of each gender? From the table, there are 90 anxious pupils out of 154, that is, 58.4%. If that applied equally to boys and girls, you would expect 58.4% of 81 boys to express anxiety (47.3) and 58.4% of 73 girls (42.7). But what you observe in practice is not what you expect:

| | What you observed | | What you expected | |
	Anxious	Not Anxious	Anxious	Not Anxious
Boys	44.0	37.0	47.3	33.7
Girls	46.0	27.0	42.7	30.3

So, there is a small difference between what you find and what you would expect if 'transfer anxiety' were equally distributed. The key to chi-squared testing is this comparison of observed and expected numbers. The test calculates the differences and applies procedures that allow for the size of the sample. We will illustrate this using the figures above and, for comparison, a set with the same proportions but a sample ten times larger:

| | What you observed | | What you expected | |
	Anxious	Not Anxious	Anxious	Not Anxious
Boys	440	370	473	337
Girls	460	270	427	303

Step 1. The first step is to calculate the differences between observed and expected numbers for each item in the table. This is usually expressed by the formula $(O - E)$. For our anxious boys, it is $44.0 - 47.3$, or -3.3. Overall, we get:

| | 'Our' results | | 'Ten times' results | |
	Anxious	Not Anxious	Anxious	Not Anxious
Boys	–3.3	3.3	–33	33
Girls	3.3	–3.3	33	–33

You will notice that in each table the numbers are all the same, but half are plus and half minus. This makes sense: if there are fewer anxious boys than we expected, there are bound to be correspondingly more non-anxious boys. (This means that as soon as we calculate any one difference we could fill in the rest of that table: in statistical terms we have 'one degree of freedom'.)

Step 2. You calculate the square of each number: this gives you $(O - E)^2$. This is a common device in statistics for getting rid of negative signs so that numbers can then be added together without cancelling out. Here it also exaggerates the 'sample size' effect: the figures in the 'ten times' table are now 100 times greater.

	'Our' results		'Ten times' results	
	Anxious	Not Anxious	Anxious	Not Anxious
Boys	10.89	10.89	1089	1089
Girls	10.89	10.89	1089	1089

Step 3. Divide each number by the expected figure for that item. This gives you $(O – E)^2 ÷ E$. For our anxious boys we have $10.89 ÷ 47.3$, or 0.230; for the large sample we have $1089 ÷ 473$, or 2.30. This removes the exaggeration of the 'sample size' effect. It gives us four different numbers in each table: thus our anxious boys score 0.230, while the not-anxious girls score 0.359. This reflects the fact that the difference for the boys was 3.3 out of 47.3 (about 7%) while for the girls it was 3.3 out of only 30.3 (nearly 11%), and so, in proportion, it is more significant. Overall we have:

	'Our' results		'Ten times' results	
	Anxious	Not Anxious	Anxious	Not Anxious
Boys	0.230	0.322	2.30	3.22
Girls	0.254	0.359	2.54	3.59

Step 4. Add together the four numbers in the table:

'Our' results: $0.230 + 0.322 + 0.254 + 0.359 = 1.165$

'Ten times' results: $2.30 + 3.22 + 2.54 + 3.59 = 11.65$

Step 5. Look up the result in a table showing the distribution of χ^2 values. We have included a basic one at the back of this book. They usually list 'degrees of freedom' (*df*) in one direction, running from 1 to 30; and 'probability' (P), in the other, running from 0.90 down to 0.01 or less. We have one degree of freedom and opposite that you will find that our value of 1.165 lies above $P = 0.10$.

What does this mean? It means that there is a difference but you cannot be sure that it represents a difference between boys and girls generally, rather than just the particular boys and girls that you happen to be dealing with on this occasion. There is a possibility (greater than 10%) that the difference is just a one-off chance.

By comparison, the 'ten times' result of 11.65 would correspond to a probability of below 0.001; that is, the odds against getting the result by chance are less than 1 in 1000. This reinforces the point made in Chapter 2 that the degree of certainty you can attach to any results depends, statistically, mainly on the numbers in your sample. With small numbers, a large difference may not reach statistical significance and you should consider other ways of convincing people that it is 'real'. With large numbers, even a small difference may be *statistically* significant, but you would have to consider whether it was of any *educational* significance.

You could apply a similar test to pupils from different associated primary schools. Again, you would start by supposing that the proportion of 'anxious' pupils is the same (58.4%) for all associated primaries: for A it is 58.4% of 47 (27.5) and so on. What you predict is not what you find.

	A	B	C	D	E	F
Expected	27.5	21.0	13.4	8.2	8.2	11.7
Observed	10.0	17.0	22.0	13.0	12.0	16.0

Here the differences are much larger in proportion to the numbers you are dealing with. Chi-squared calculates out at 56.6. The larger table has more degrees of freedom, which can be calculated for any table by the formula:

$$(\text{Number of rows} - 1) \times (\text{Number of columns} - 1)$$

In the present case we have two rows (anxious and non-anxious) and six columns (schools A to F) and so we have five degrees of freedom: $(2-1) \times (6-1)$. You can see how the formula comes about: in this case if you fill in five of the columns in one of the rows, you can then work out all the other figures, since you know the totals for each row and column.

When we look up the chi-squared values opposite five degrees of freedom, we find that the possibility of this being a chance event is quite negligible: less than 1 in 100,000,000,000...

Summary

This chapter has described the main stages in analysing data. There are four simple and straightforward steps you can take to make description of the data thorough and systematic. These are:

- Prepare a grid
- Design a simple coding system
- Check the validity and reliability of your coding system for open questions by asking a friend to code a sample of the data
- Know in advance how you are going to code missing data. Code 'don't know' and 'no data' differently.

Once all your data is entered on the grid, it is a simple matter to count up the different kinds of answers to your original questions on the questionnaire. At this stage of description remember:

- Do not read anything into the data that is not there
- Calculate responses in terms of numbers who answered the question not in terms of the total sample
- You are not measuring anything and so 'averages' and 'standard deviation' are not appropriate
- A simple statistical test such as chi-squared can tell you if your findings are significant.

Going beyond description to begin interpreting the data, you may want to compare groups or answers in two or more columns.

Remember:

- Do not confuse opinions with an attribute of the thing you are asking about – in the raspberry yoghurt example, opinions given tell you about people's taste, not the yoghurt
- Be prepared for a hypothesis to be disproved: you *can* be wrong
- Think about the implications of your data: answer the 'So what?' question.

In the final chapter we consider interpreting data in more detail.

6

So What? Interpreting, Presenting and Using the Results

You are now at the happy stage of having constructed your questionnaire, piloted it, used it, and have analysed the responses. Where to you go from here? The answer to this deceptively simple question depends on the context in which you are working. You need to decide:

- What the important results are
- Who is to be told about the results
- How to present the results
- The changes (if any) suggested by the results.

This chapter deals with each of these matters in turn. It does not present a guaranteed recipe for research to influence policy and practice. If only life were that simple! Rather it identifies matters to be considered for your research to have most impact.

Deciding what is important

As we saw in Chapter 5, there are two key stages in analysing data. The first involves describing the data. Here, you collect together the information you have gathered about, for example, pupils' anxieties about transferring from primary to secondary school. You could describe the data in terms of:

- Total number of pupils expressing anxiety
- Numbers of pupils expressing anxiety per associated primary
- Kinds of anxieties experienced by pupils
- Numbers of boys and girls expressing anxiety.

These are examples of some of the ways in which you might organise your data, imposing an order on the information.

The second stage is interpreting the data. This means drawing out the important points from the description. It can be helpful to think of this stage as answering the question 'So what?' once you have organised the data. Suppose the data reveal that 98% of pupils transferring to secondary school expressed anxiety of one kind or another. So what? One interpretation could be that the primary/secondary liaison policy needed rethinking, assuming, of course, that its intention was to minimise anxiety. Again, if your data revealed that most pupils were particularly anxious about finding their way around the school, the answer to 'So what?' might be ways of alleviating this – such as better signposting, having older pupils around as guides, being forgiving of new pupils arriving late for lessons and so on. Note in this example that 'So what?' has two elements to it:

(1) The school should do something
(2) What it is that ought to be done.

The first of these is directly connected to the data; the second is your notion of what could be done. It is important to keep this distinction clear when you are presenting your results. You need to be clear about what is firmly rooted in your data and what are your ideas and suggestions, stimulated by the data but not tested by collecting evidence. In other words, in the above example, you had not asked pupils whether they would find better signposting helpful.

There is no magic formula for interpreting the data. Discussion with colleagues helps develop ideas: it can be useful, if painful, to discuss your interpretation with sceptical and critical colleagues. Sometimes an alternative interpretation clarifies your own thoughts. The important point to stress is that interpretation is based on evidence, systematically collected and analysed. It is not the same as intuition or a hunch.

Once you are clear in your own mind what you want to say, you need then to decide who is to be told. In practice, of course, these two things are closely interconnected. If you have been researching primary-to-secondary school transfer, you know you will be reporting back something to the primaries and something to the secondary school involved. If your interpretation of your findings suggests that changes need to be made then the question of the audience for your findings is critical.

Audience

Attention is more likely to be paid to your findings if you have done the groundwork in advance. Better always to talk through the possibilities of an investigation and where you hope it will lead, before you start. One of the many advantages of team research is that findings are more likely to be taken seriously simply because a group of teachers has been sufficiently concerned about a problem to research it. Beyond this, it is important to get the support of the key people likely to be affected by your research before you start. An example brings this home. Suppose you are researching primary/secondary liaison procedures and have not discussed this with the key staff involved. You breeze into the staffroom announcing that you have evidence that liaison is a complete shambles. All this does is put people's backs up, encourages them to adopt a defensive attitude and become highly resistant to changing primary/secondary liaison procedures, no matter how competent and convincing your research. The ideal situation would be one where the key staff involved recognised that there was a problem with primary/secondary liaison procedures, worked out, as a group, the key aspects to be investigated (the research questions), were involved in constructing or commenting on the questionnaire, and so were predisposed to think about and act on the findings.

It is essential that the purposes of the research are discussed with the key people likely to be affected by it before the research begins. You need the support of interested parties if the research is to have any impact. Clearly people directly affected by the research and those who are likely to influence change are key audiences.

You also need to think through whether there is anything sensitive or embarrassing in your findings and, if so, what the implications are for publicising them. Suppose, for example, that pupils from one primary school express markedly more anxieties about transfer than pupils from all other primaries put together.

Who needs to know this? Do all the associated primaries need to know, for example? The answer to this depends on a whole range of factors, such as the relationships amongst primary headteachers, the kinds of anxieties expressed, the kind of developments in policy that are suggested, the role of the primary adviser. All we are stressing here is that you consider carefully who the audience for your findings needs to be as well as the findings themselves.

Presenting the results

It is a truism that more time and effort is spent on thinking through and doing the research than in planning its dissemination; yet communicating the results of research is as important as the research itself. In presenting results you are trying to do two different things:

- Open your findings to scrutiny and so to validation
- Persuade people to a certain point of view.

You need to be clear in your own mind about:

- The points you want to get across to a particular audience – remembering that you may want to get across different points to different audiences
- The evidence which led you to identify the points, thereby letting the audience judge the validity of these points.

The following questions are offered for you to consider when you come to present your findings. There are no right answers.

- Which forms of presentation are you going to use – written report, oral presentation, discussion group?
- If you are presenting findings orally, how long do you need? Be brief – 15 to 20 minutes will endear you to your audience and there are limits to the number of points an audience can take in. What is it that you really want them to remember?
- In an oral presentation or a discussion group would it be helpful to let the audience have some written backup material? A copy of key points is useful for keeping you and the audience on track.

- When is the best time to present findings? Don't feel you have to rush into print or talk to the staff or pupils as soon as the work is finished. Timing may be important. When is the audience likely to be most receptive? Avoid last thing on a Friday, ends of term and exceptionally busy times of year. It can also be helpful to put your report on ice for a little time. This helps to give you critical distance on what you've written.
- What kind of information are you going to pass back to those who took the time and trouble to complete the questionnaire? When?

Tables, bar charts and pie charts

It is likely that you will want to present your findings using some or all of these. The first thing to remember is that a certain amount of selectivity is inevitable. It would be unwise to overwhelm your audience with all the information you have collected. As we stressed above, you need to think hard, and argue through, what the important information is and why it is important. The second point to remember is that you want to enlighten your audience, not mystify them.

With tables it is helpful in most circumstances to round figures to the nearest whole number, particularly if there is a long list. Compare Tables 1A and 1B (overleaf):

Table 1A: Percentage of pupils expressing anxiety about coming to secondary school by primary school

	Boys	Girls
Primary A	23.07	19.04
Primary B	47.61	46.66
Primary C	88.88	100.00
Primary D	100.00	90.00
Primary E	84.61	100.00
Primary F	62.50	91.66

Table 1B: Percentage of pupils expressing anxiety about coming to secondary school (to nearest whole number)

	Boys	Girls
Primary A	23	19
Primary B	48	47
Primary C	89	100
Primary D	100	90
Primary E	85	100
Primary F	63	92

Table 1B is easier to read. By presenting figures to nearest whole numbers you are also deciding that percentage points are not important for your interpretation of the results and so are not important for the reader as validation. You should also consider whether you should use numbers or percentages. Percentages are misleading if you are dealing with small numbers. In Table 1B, above, 100% of girls from Primary E were anxious about coming to secondary school. Table 2 shows that this meant one girl was anxious.

Table 2: Numbers of pupils expressing anxiety about coming to secondary school

	Boys	(Total)	%	Girls	(Total)	%	
Primary A	6	(26)	23	4	(21)	19	
Primary B	10	(21)	48	7	(15)	47	
Primary C	8	(9)	89	14	(14)	100	
Primary D	4	4	100	9	10	90	
Primary E	11	13	85	1	1	100	
Primary F	5	8	63	11	12	92	
Totals	44	81		46	73		154

Table 2, however, looks messy and the information it contains could be conveyed more effectively. How you do this depends on your research questions. For example, if the main purpose of the research is to find out how many pupils transferring from primary are anxious, you simply say that 90 out of 154 express some kind of anxiety. In our view it is easier and simpler to stick to numbers rather than use percentages in these circumstances, particularly if you want to indicate the numbers of boys and girls expressing anxiety. As soon as you get numbers below 100 it is safer not to use percentages.

If you want to do more than this and convey the proportions of pupils coming from the six primary schools expressing anxiety, then a bar graph or pie chart can convey this quite effectively. You do not get the precise percentages in these forms but you do get an overall impression of proportion. Figure 1 shows more immediately the numbers of pupils anxious and not anxious in each primary school. In School A, for example, 10 pupils are anxious and 36 are not anxious.

Figure 1: Anxiety about transfer to secondary (1)

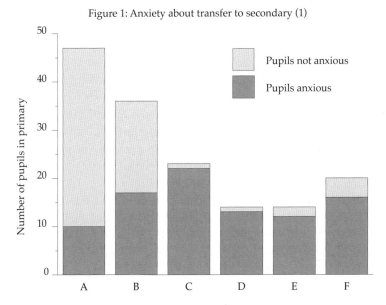

Suppose, however, that your research question concerns gender differences among pupils expressing anxiety and that you want to look at this in terms of primary school attended. Figure 2 would do the trick. For example, of the ten anxious pupils School A sends to secondary, six are boys and four are girls.

Figure 2: Anxiety about transfer to secondary (2)

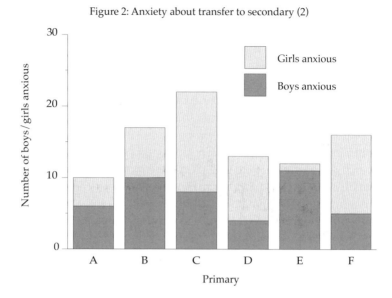

Figure 2 conveys at a glance that School C sends over 20 anxious pupils to secondary school. It also seems to have the largest number of girls expressing anxiety. What it hides is the proportion of children from each school coming to secondary who are anxious, and the proportion of the pupils from each that make up the secondary's total first year intake. In fact School C sends 23 pupils to the secondary, about 15% of the total intake. So, in presenting your information about gender differences and primaries, it would be wise to begin with basic information about the proportions of the total first year intake coming from each primary as in Figure 1 and then move on to Figure 2. Everything hinges on what the focus of your research is. Before leaving this topic it is worthwhile emphasising that different messages are conveyed by the way you present data and that it is best to avoid percentages when dealing with small numbers.

Take, for example, Figures 2 and 3, which present exactly the same data. Figure 2 presents the data in terms of numbers but hides the proportion of pupils sent to the secondary by each primary school. However it shows that Schools C, B and F all send more than 15 anxious pupils to the secondary school. It identifies School C as a priority for further investigation.

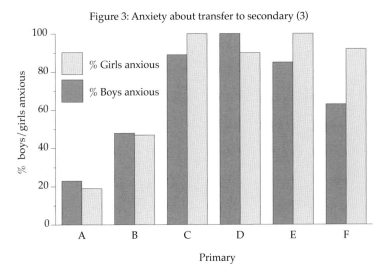

Figure 3: Anxiety about transfer to secondary (3)

Figure 3 presents the same information in percentages. In our view the information in Figure 3 is less useful precisely because it hides the numbers involved and does not target schools for further investigation. Schools C, D, E and F all look worrying, but School B might escape notice even though it sent more anxious pupils to the secondary than Schools D, E and F.

So far we have concentrated on presenting information about the numbers of pupils expressing anxiety. Let us now consider how to present information about the kinds of anxieties expressed by pupils. You could do this using a table.

Table 3: Kinds of anxiety

Kinds of anxiety	Number of pupils
Work will be hard	47
Big school	30
New teachers	18
No anxiety	59

This is perfectly acceptable, but consider the same information presented as a pie chart.

Table 7: Pupils expressing anxieties

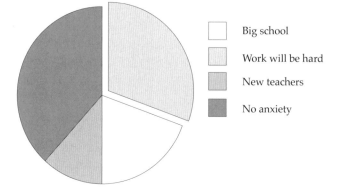

Big school

Work will be hard

New teachers

No anxiety

Do you agree that it conveys the information more effectively than the table? It is always worth considering a pie chart when you are dealing with a fixed amount – 100% – and want to show how this 100% is divided up. It is useful if you are dealing with a small number of divisions, three or four. Once you get much above this, the chart can become cluttered and difficult to interpret. All these bar charts and pie charts can be produced using easily available spreadsheet and word processor applications.

Recommending changes

So far we have been concentrating on presenting information for validation; in other words, saying to your audience, 'Here is the evidence which has led me to the following conclusions'. It may be that your conclusions will suggest the need for some kind of change or development of school policy and practice.

If there are changes or developments suggested by your results it is important to be clear about those which are in the school's power to do something about and those which lie outwith the school's influence. To continue with the primary/secondary liaison example, there may be things that only the primary schools can do and things that only the secondary school can do. Hundreds of books have been written about how change occurs in schools.

Here we will confine ourselves to making three common-sense points about change:

- People generally need an *incentive* to change. If the school policy has been such and such for years, or something has always been done in a certain way, why should people change their routine practice? What is in it for them? In advocating a change, therefore, you need to be clear how this change will make life better or easier.
- People feel threatened by change. If you have to do something differently or do something that you've never done before it can expose you to failure. Nobody enjoys failing – a risk which trying a new teaching method, setting up new administrative systems, or introducing new courses always carries.
- Change is difficult to bring about. Ask yourself seriously, 'Does my evidence suggest that change is needed? Does it indicate what kind of change would be beneficial?' Remember the old American folk saying, 'If it ain't broke, don't fix it.'

Not all research suggests changes are needed. If you are using a questionnaire to evaluate a course, for example, it may well be that your respondents are well satisfied with the content and teaching approach. It is important to remember that research can provide positive reinforcement of a well-designed and thoughtful programme or policy. It should not always be associated with deficits.

Finally...

Beware of being convinced that you have the truth. All research is fallible and at best you have a glimpse of the way things are. Most research leaves you feeling that you need to know more, and can raise new areas that need investigation. We do not say this to put you off the whole business of doing research. On the contrary, we hope that research will be an enjoyable, interesting and stimulating activity that will whet your appetite for more. Its ultimate justification is that it leads to school improvement and professional development. Although research carried out by teachers, by choice, towards these ends may not provide straightforward answers about school improvement, it *can* help you to understand why things are the way they are, and make you better informed about the implications of taking one course of action rather than another. The knowledge revealed by your research is inevitably incomplete but it can and does lead to improving the quality of education.

Further Reading

There are many excellent texts on research methods for those wishing to pursue their interest in questionnaires. Here are a few as starting points.

The standard work in this field is:
Oppenheim, A. N. (2000) *Questionnaire Design, Interviewing and Attitude Measurement.* Continuum.

Another useful text is:
Moser, C. A. & Kalton, G. (1985) *Survey Methods in Social Investigation.* Ashgate.

A readable chapter on survey design is contained in:
Cohen, L., Manion, L. & Morrison, K. (2000) *Research Methods in Education.* 5th edition. RoutledgeFalmer.

The above also provide good lists of further reading on specific aspects of surveys, such as sampling and statistical analysis.

An easy-to-read book about using statistics is:
Rowntree, D. (2003) *Statistics Without Tears: A primer for non-mathematicians.* Allyn & Bacon.

General books for teachers on doing research are:
Bell, J. (1999) *Doing Your Research Project.* 3rd edition. Open University Press.

O'Hanlon, C. (ed.)(1996) *Professional Development through Action Research.* RoutledgeFalmer. (This is one of a large number of books on action research and reflective practice. It describes ways of using action research to improve teaching and learning.)

A guide to formulating research questions is the first booklet of the SCRE *Using Research* series:
Lewis, I. & Munn, P. (2004) *So You Want To Do Research! A guide for beginners on how to formulate research questions.* 2nd revised edition. Edinburgh: SCRE Centre.

Values of Chi-Squared (χ^2)*

df	Probability (P)		
	0.10	0.05	0.01
1	2.71	3.84	6.64
2	4.60	5.99	9.21
3	6.25	7.82	11.34
4	7.78	9.49	13.28
5	9.24	11.07	15.09
6	10.64	12.59	16.81
7	12.02	14.07	18.48
8	13.36	15.51	20.09
9	14.68	16.92	21.67
10	15.99	18.31	23.21
11	17.28	19.68	24.72
12	18.55	21.03	26.22
13	19.81	22.36	27.69
14	21.06	23.68	29.14
15	22.31	25.00	30.58
16	23.54	26.30	32.00
17	24.77	27.59	33.41
18	25.99	28.87	34.80
19	27.20	30.14	36.19
20	28.41	31.41	37.57
21	29.62	32.67	38.93
22	30.81	33.92	40.29
23	32.01	35.17	41.64
24	33.20	36.42	42.98
25	34.38	37.65	44.31
26	35.56	38.88	45.64
27	36.74	40.11	46.96
28	37.92	41.34	48.28
29	39.09	42.56	49.59
30	40.26	43.77	50.89

* Selected values only. See, for example, Fisher, R. and Yates, F. (1974) *Statistical tables for biological, agricultural and medical research* (Longman) for a more comprehensive range of values.